Teen Love:
A Journal
On Relationships

A Journal
On Relationships

Kimberly Kirberger

With Colin Mortensen from MTV's
The Real World Hawaii

Health Communications, Inc.
Deerfield Beach, Florida

www.hci-online.com

We would like to acknowledge the many publishers and individuals who granted us permission to reprint the cited material. (Note: The stories that were penned anonymously, that are in the public domain, or that were written by Kimberly Kirberger are not included in this listing.)

All material in *Colin's Pages* is by Colin Mortensen. Reprinted by permission of Colin Mortensen. ©1999 Colin Mortensen.

Dear Boy. Reprinted by permission of Sarah Bercot. ©1999 Sarah Bercot.

Dear Girl. Reprinted by permission of Derek Whittier. ©1999 Derek Whittier.

My Solemn Friend. Reprinted by permission of Lindsey Hartman. ©1999 Lindsey Hartman.

My Best Feature. Reprinted by permission of Sara Nachtman. ©1999 Sara Nachtman.

Falling. Reprinted by permission of Christina Atkinson. ©1999 Christina Atkinson.

(Continued on page 207)

Publisher: Health Communications, Inc.
　　　　　 3201 S.W. 15th Street
　　　　　 Deerfield Beach, FL 33442-8190

Cover and inside book design by Lawna Patterson Oldfield

To my husband,
John, and my son, Jesse.
Thanks for all you have taught me
about love, and for being a safe
place to keep my
heart open.

Contents

3. All These New Feelings

4. There Is a First Time for Everything

5. Do You Like Me?

6. When Friends Become More

7. Unrequited Love

8. Now That We're Together

9. Breaking Up Is Hard to Do

10. Starting Over

Acknowledgments

Someone once told me that although each of us has potential to accomplish our goals it really makes a difference if someone believes in you and tells you that you can do it. For me, that person was—and is—my brother, Jack Canfield. I will always be grateful to him. Jack was one of the first people to work for self-esteem for young people, and much of his work is passed on in these pages.

My parents are two of the kindest and most supportive people I know. They gave me great confidence and guided me brilliantly throughout my teen years and loves.

There are two incredible people who helped so much with this book: Tasha Boucher and Mitch Claspy are the reason this got to my publisher on time and in almost perfect shape. This book would not have been possible without them. My gratitude cannot be expressed in words. Tasha and Mitch, I love you both.

My son, Jesse, teaches me so much about what it is like to be a teenager. He also teaches me about unconditional love, which is by far the best love of all.

My husband, John, is my partner and my best friend. We have shared a long and sometimes difficult journey together, but we know that every difficulty that we get through opens the door to a better and sweeter togetherness.

My publisher, Peter Vegso, has been so supportive. I thank him for believing in me and trusting that this series would be well received. I hope I never let him down.

Larry Getlen, Randee Feldman, Laine Latimer, Kelly Maragni and Kim Weiss have worked so hard to make sure that teens everywhere know about this series. Thanks for being so much fun to work with, for being so creative and for making me look so good.

Matthew Diener and Lisa Drucker are both so wonderful to work with. They make the editing process run smoothly, yet they don't miss anything. I know I am lucky to have these two as my editors.

I want to thank Colin Mortensen for believing in the work I am doing and signing on. His perspective and his involvement bring a new life to the project that is positive and fun.

Nina Palais, thank you for keeping the Teen Letter Project running so smoothly. What you do is so important.

Thank you to Jessie Braun, Lia Gay and Becca Woolf for their editorial and creative input on this workbook.

Thanks to our "in-house" teens for making sure that everything we do is on target. Thank you Dawn Geer, Elliot Hallmark, Kelly Harrington, Rose Lannutti, Lindsay Ross and Lisa Rothbard for being the vital force in our offices.

Kimberly Kirberger

To my mom and dad, the two best parents in the world. Mom, your beauty, love, strength and intelligence have made me a better person; your influence on me is tremendously positive and unendingly appreciated. Thank you for always being there when I need you. Dad, your love, wit, support and guidance in my everyday life are remarkable. I can always count on you, and not many people have that in a father. I cherish it.

To my brother, Ryan, you are everything I am not and I admire all of you—your sweet sensitive nature, your artistic inclination, your unconditional support. You were there to lead the way for me as my older brother and friend, to show me what I could and couldn't do. You deserve all the happiness in the world and I know you will have it, you're too nice, loving and well-meaning not to. I love you, Ryan.

To Trevor and Mike, you guys are my best friends and soul mates. I don't know where I would be without you two (definitely not on the cover of this book). I hope we grow old together!

Casey, you knew we were both gonna wreck @#$% up.

Michelle, *Wuf Wuf!*

Grandma, I wish I could pinch your cheek right now.

Fritz, you are a wonderful grandfather, and I love you.

Joey, stay cute.

Casey C., thanks for the advice about the hair.

Talal and Nick, stop lying.

Max, grow up.

Summer, be independent and strong.

Kelly, have a rad summer!

Jessie, go Bruins.

Colin Mortensen

 Introduction

*D*ear Friend,

As I write this, my heart is filled with excitement and compassion for you. You are embarking on such a wonderful time of life, one that is filled with lessons and love, heartbreak and ecstasy. You are discovering the world of romantic love.

This journal has been designed to be a helping hand through all of this. By writing down your thoughts and feelings you return to yourself. By returning to yourself you grow and become stronger and wiser. There is no experience that will break you. Everything will only serve to make you stronger. By writing things down you cleanse your heart, leaving it pure and open to new and wonderful experiences.

Let this journal be your friend and let it help you to remember that all of your experiences are for your learning. By remembering this, all experiences become positive ones.

My heart is with you as you embark on this journey. I wish for you to always remember how wonderful you are and to remember when you hear your own heart beating it is to remind you that you are loved completely.

Have fun and enjoy your journey!

[AUTHOR'S NOTE: *The next book in this series is* Teen Love: On Friendship. *Please send us stories, poems and questions you want answered about friendship. Also please send us any comments and/or suggestions.*]

Dear Boy

Dear Boy,

I do not know who you are, or where or when we will meet, but I do hope it is soon.

I pray that when we meet and fall in love, you will love me for me, and not hope for someone who is thinner or prettier. I hope you won't compare me to girls who may have brighter smiles or better grades, or who can jump higher. I hope that you will make me laugh, take care of me if I get sick, and be trustworthy.

I hope you will remember that I prefer daisies to roses, and that my favorite color changes with my mood. Please know that my eyes aren't blue; they're gray, with flecks of navy.

Please know that I might be too shy to kiss you first, but please don't be afraid. I won't slap you or push you away. I'm sure your kisses will be perfect. When we go on a date, please don't stress about where to take me; what's important is that I'm with you.

If I cry, please know it isn't because of you; just hold me close and I'll heal quickly. And, if it is because of you, I'll heal just the same.

And if we decide to break up, please understand that I may be bitter, but I'd like to be your friend if you'll let me. I promise to remember that you have feelings, too, even though you'll never admit it, and when you are ready, we'll have a "special friendship."

Please tell me if anything I do bothers you, or if something just doesn't sit right. I would like you to always be honest with me. If I have a bad day, I hope you will shower me with confidence and smiles.

I hope you don't think that I'm asking too much of you. I hope you understand that I'm a little bit nervous and very scared. I wish I could tell you how or when we will meet, and if we will be in love forever. Every relationship is a new game of cards, and . . . *(sigh)* . . . I've never been good at cards. But I will try my best to be kind and love you dearly for all that you are, without expecting too much from you. Thank you for listening—this is all that I ask.

Yours always,
Sarah

Sarah Bercot

Dear Girl

Dear Girl,

I feel that the time has come for me to have a girlfriend. I know you're out there somewhere. Don't worry, I'll find you.

And when I do, I hope that you will love me because I'm Derek, not because I'm Mike's younger brother. I hope that you won't be embarrassed when my clothes don't match, or be annoyed when I want to watch the Lakers on ESPN, and not *Party of Five*.

I hope that you will remember I play soccer, not football, and that I play midfield, not defense, and that every weekend I live with my dad.

I pray that you'll love me despite my tendency to forget birthdays, and if your parents invite me to dinner please write their names really small on my hand so I can use it as reference.

Please know that I will constantly act strong and in control, but realize that inside I am lost and confused. (Just don't tell my friends.) Please don't worry if I hurt myself skateboarding. Instead, be there to mend my wounds with kisses.

Understand that loving each other means being together, but not all the time. We should never bail on our friends. Also understand that I may at times act jealous, and overly protective, but only because *I* have insecurities, not because *you* are doing anything wrong.

And if we fall out of love with one another, please don't hate me. And if I cry in front of you, please don't laugh at me. Please know that I am sensitive . . . in a manly tough kind of way.

Please be honest with me without being hurtful. After all I am a *boy.* And I promise to always be honest with you, because you deserve honesty. And I promise to open doors for you, and buy your ticket when we go to the movies.

And, no, you aren't fat, so please don't constantly ask, and you don't need makeup either. Oh, and don't be upset if you cut your hair and I don't notice. I will love you even in Levi's and a T-shirt.

I hope you don't think I'm asking too much of you. I just want to be happy making you happy. I'm coming to find you, so don't go anywhere, stay where you are, whoever you are. And by the way, my name's Derek.

Yours always,

Derek

Derek Whittier

My Solemn Friend

Expressing my feelings comes easily,
When voices I cannot hear.
If I try to talk to someone,
Rejection is my fear.
So on this piece of paper,
I write to my solemn friend.
Every small detail,
Each enormous sin.
Some of my words sing with joy,
Warming the coldest heart.
Others scream with rage
Each word a poison dart.
I do not need a long lecture,
Or any words of advice.
That's why I stick to paper,
It lets me lead my life.
Paper does not judge me,
Or offer a cliché.
When I'm finished writing,
There are no looks of dismay.
Paper has no choice but to listen,
And record every thought.
Plus, I can always look back,
And read lessons I've been
taught.

Lindsey Hartman

one

Love Yourself First

To love oneself is the beginning
of a lifelong romance.

Oscar Wilde

Love Yourself First

The most important relationship you will ever have is the one you have with yourself. How you feel about yourself will affect how others feel about you. It will affect the way you let others treat you and most of all it will define the way you treat yourself.

We all want to be loved and we focus most of our attention on the outside to earn that love. I am constantly behaving in ways that I think will make people love me. What we all need to remember is that love must first come from inside.

I cannot control how others think about me.

I cannot control how others treat me.

I certainly cannot control how much others love me.

BUT:

I can love myself.

I can treat myself better.

I can choose the things I say to myself and how I think of myself.

I can try each day to open my heart to myself.

In order to begin the process of becoming your own best friend it is necessary to observe how you treat yourself and how you talk to yourself.

♥ How do you think of yourself? List ten positive things you think about yourself:

For example:
I am attractive; I am nice, etc.

1. _____
2. _____
3. _____
4. _____
5. _____
6. _____
7. _____
8. _____
9. _____
10. _____

♥ List the first ten negative things you think about yourself (no editing!):

For example:

I am overweight; I am a coward, etc.

1. _____

2. _____

3. _____

4. _____

5. _____

6. _____

7. _____

8. _____

9. _____

10. _____

> There are no perfect beings and
> there never will be.
>
> Henry Miller

$\mathcal{M}$any people think the goal is to have all the qualities of the first list and to completely eliminate those traits from the second one. Not only is this an unrealistic goal but it is an unhealthy one as well. Part of what endears us to others is our vulnerability. Can you imagine having a friend who is perfect?

If there are things on the negative list that are harmful, like "I steal," then of course this is something you want to try to change. But if some of those things are "My nose is too big" or "My feelings get hurt easily," these are qualities that make you who you are, and the job is not to get rid of them, but to accept them.

♥ Now make a list of all the qualities you accept in yourself—the good, the bad and the ugly:

1. _____

2. _____

3. _____

4. _____

5. _____

6. _____

7. _____

8. _____

9. _____

10. _____

The curious paradox is that when I accept
myself just as I am, I can change.

Carl Rogers

As we learn to accept ourselves more we begin to treat *ourselves better.* Promise yourself that each day you will do things specifically for you.

♥ Make a list of things that make you happy, things that are healthy for you, things that make you feel more attractive, or things that help you to be more physically fit:

1. _____

2. _____

3. _____

4. _____

5. _____

6. _____

7. _____

8. _____

9. _____

10. _____

11. _____

12. _____

13. _____

14. _____

15. _____

16. _____

17. _____

18. _____

The goal is to do as many things from this list as possible each day. (Don't overdo it!) Put a check next to the things you do each day.

If you do this exercise you will notice a change in how you think about yourself and how others respond to you immediately. The more it becomes a daily habit, the more you are on your way to a very special, lifelong friendship . . . with yourself.

There is no one, no one, who loves you like yourself.

Brendan Behan

♥ After you have had time to let all this sink in and have begun to do the exercises, return here and write about your experience:

_____

_____

_____

_____

_____

_____

_____

_____

_____

_____

_____

_____

_____

♥ Take a picture of yourself before you begin the process of treating yourself better. After a couple of months do an "after" picture.

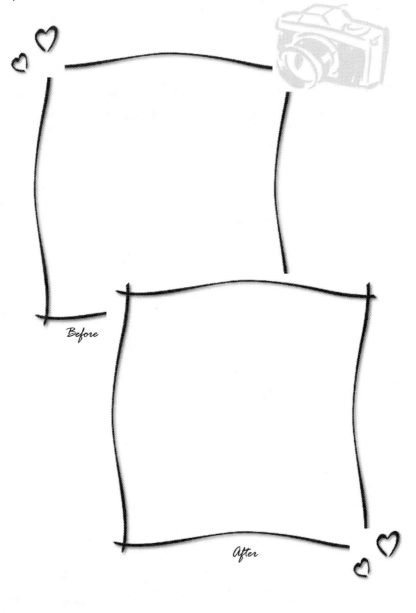

Before

After

Best Friend's Pages

My Best Friend

♥ Have your best friend write all the things that she or he likes about you:

_____

_____

_____

_____

_____

_____

_____

♥ Have your best friend write about the changes she or he sees in you since you began treating yourself better:

_____

_____

_____

_____

_____

_____

_____

_____

_____

_____

_____

_____

_____

_____

_____

_____

♥ Have your best friend make a list of all the qualities that make you lovable:

1. _____

2. _____

3. _____

4. _____

5. _____

6. _____

7. _____

8. _____

9. _____

10. _____

There are two ways of spreading light:
to be the candle or the mirror
that reflects it.

Edith Wharton

Colin's Pages

Loving Yourself

*L*ove yourself enough to treat yourself right. Your friends, family, and boyfriend or girlfriend will take your lead and treat you the way they see you treating yourself.

If you aren't being treated with love and respect, then walk away. I have seen so many people that I care about get caught up in a bad relationship because they are insecure and don't believe they deserve better. YOU DESERVE BETTER . . . PERIOD.

I have also seen my friends act on their insecurities by doing anything they could to please their boyfriend or girlfriend. (You know, when a person talks and always refers to what his or her girlfriend/boyfriend wants and you never hear that person mention his or her own needs?) I think it is a big mistake to believe that love means putting someone else's needs and happiness before your own. It is great to care, but not to care so much that by doing so you compromise your own needs.

I have a very close friend who had a very controlling boyfriend. She was always walking on eggshells, petrified of doing something that would make him angry. He used his "love" as a means for control, always threatening to take it away if she didn't behave according to his desires. It was so sad and so hard for me to watch someone I cared about go through this. It was like she was disappearing a little every

day, and by the end of the
school year she didn't even
know who she was, let
alone what she needed.

   She did eventually
end the relationship and
it was horribly painful for
her to look back and see
what she had compromised
and what she had missed by
allowing herself to be controlled
by this guy. Her message to you right now would be: If you
find yourself in a relationship with someone who tries to control you and make you feel like you are worthless without him
or her, get out now. That person will not change. It will not
get better if you just _____

_____

(fill in the blank). That's what you get caught up in thinking. If
I treat him better then he won't be so angry with me all the
time. Or, he just loves me so much that he can't handle it
when I hang out with my girlfriends. THAT IS NOT LOVE!!!!!

   Remember that you are perfect . . . you are great just the
way you are and you deserve to be treated with love and
respect. No less . . . no matter what. *No less . . . no matter
what.*

Colin

Colin's Questions

♥ Have you ever been involved in an abusive relationship? This includes emotional, intellectual, verbal or physical abuse.

☐ Yes ☐ No

♥ If yes, did you stay with the person? ☐ Yes ☐ No

♥ What made you stay?

_____

_____

_____

_____

_____

_____

_____

_____

_____

♥ How did it finally end?

_____

_____

_____

_____

_____

_____

_____

♥ Do you think you deserve
someone who will treat you ☐ *Yes* ☐ *No*
with respect?

♥ What does "being treated with respect" mean to you?

_____

_____

_____

_____

_____

_____

_____

♥ Make a list of ways your partner could treat you with love and respect on a daily basis:

1. _____

2. _____

3. _____

4. _____

5. _____

6. _____

7. _____

8. _____

9. _____

10. _____

*T*his poem is from the *Teen Love* book but I felt it was so good—and so important—I wanted you to read it again.

My Best Feature

I asked my friend this afternoon,
As I gazed into my reflection—
What she thought of what I saw?
She said, Images are usually misconceptions.

I started to put down my appearance,
Wishing I was thinner or taller.
She looked at me with understanding eyes—
Saying, Superficial wishes only make you smaller.
I knew she was right, but who was she to talk,
For she was every guy's dream—
Trying to point this out to her,
She replied, Appearances aren't always what they seem.

Tell me five features you admire in yourself, she said,
And I knew my troubles had just begun—
For I could see the hurt in her expression,
When I couldn't even think of one.

I could not think of a single feature I liked,
And I could feel my stomach slowly start to sink.
So I turned to my friend and simply said,
Well what do you think?

I think you're looking at it all wrong, she said
And I wish I could make it clearer.
It's what's inside you that makes you beautiful,
And not what can be seen in the mirror.

She said, You're the most loving person I know,
And I hate to watch you fall apart.
If you want to know what makes you beautiful to me?
Your best feature is your heart.

Sara Nachtman

two

Falling in Love

Your task is not to seek for love, but
merely to seek and find all the barriers within
yourself that you have built against it.

A Course in Miracles

Falling

This newfound feeling so overwhelming
You in my arms, me in yours
The childlike fancies
Music, merry-go-rounds
Cloud nine cotton candy that melts in mouths
The flutter of butterflies that melts the heart
All I see are stars.

Christina Atkinson

Falling in Love

Oh, to fall in love. There is nothing quite like it. It is one of the sweetest of all life's experiences. One thing, though, that has always fascinated me about love is that everyone has a different definition of what it is. And even though many people may act like they are all on the same page, it is seldom that two people will define love in the same way.

♥ What is your definition of love?

_____

_____

_____

_____

_____

_____

_____

_____

_____

_____

_____

This is a hip-hop song that was lovingly dedicated to Teen Love by Public Service Announcement:

Endless Love / End Less Love

Love—it is a powerful thing
Open up your heart
and let your spirit sing
It comes and goes
The highs and the lows
from the top of your head
to the tips of your toes
Sometimes found and sometimes lost
love is free but some pay the cost
It can be found in the simplest forms
Your mommy and your daddy
and the reason we're born
Family and friends from beginning to end
in order to receive one must give and send
We must love ourselves to find ourselves
But hang on and stay strong
It's been there all along
The path of our tears
is the road to our hearts
Letting go of fears
is where we must start

It's not about the physical
from the heavens all around
To our world that is visual
God is love
Love is life
The sun loves the moon
The reflection is light
Plants love the light all day until night
Relationships are opposites
that sometimes fight
That's okay and the games we play
You see, love can make you crazy
in a beautiful way
You got to love yourself
Not judge yourself
Tap into the inner
And find limitless wealth
From a teenage love
To a lifelong marriage
We must carry each other
like a horse pulls a carriage
Express your love
and do what you feel
If we lie to one another
then our love's not real
It's all right to have questions

and not always know
If we're to hold onto our love
then we must let it go
We must love our bodies
Feet, knees and nose
It's not about our image
or our choice of clothes
It's not about our image
or our choice of clothes
It's the love that's inside us
and letting it show
It's 'bout the love that's inside us
and letting it show.

Public Service Announcement
Sagana (M. Ingram)
Eufone (K. Canfield)
Pariah (J. Gray)

We asked our Web site (*http://www.teenagechickensoup. com*) visitors to tell us their definitions of love. Here are some of their answers:

♥ I think that love is something that takes over your entire soul. If you love someone, everything you do is for him or her. You try hard to fix everything that makes that person hurt, and to prolong the happy times. But what I truly think love is, is when you can forgive someone, no matter what has happened. That's true, unconditional love.

♥ I think that love is not a feeling or an emotion, but more a state of being. When you love someone, it can be different from being *in love* with someone. When you love someone you care about that person a lot. When you're in love with someone, not only do you care about him or her a lot, but you also always want to be with them, always are thinking about them, and have a connection to them on a deeper level. Kind of like your soul connects with his or hers.

♥ You can't force love unto you; the only way to get love is to love. Love is the driving force of this planet; if there weren't love there wouldn't be life.

♥ My girlfriend and I respect each other. We don't try to change each other. We accept each other for who we are.

♥ Love isn't that great, it's just okay. Unconditional love is much better!

♥ Love is something that you feel in your heart.

♥ I think that the Greeks got it right! They have four types of love: *Eros, Storge, Philia* and *Agape. Eros* is sexual love, *Storge* is affection for family members and relatives, *Philia* is the love which is expressed in marriages and friend-ships, and *Agape* is love for all people, actively seeking their welfare.

♥ Love transcends all things, understands all things and accepts all things.

♥ Love is something that you share with someone else, whom you totally trust and admire. Love is where not only do you

♡♡♡♡♡♡♡♡♡♡♡♡♡♡♡♡♡

learn something from him or her, but also where you two would be able to gain experience of life together. Love is companionship: being best friends with the person you love and knowing that you are being loved the same way you give love.

♥ Love is appreciating someone for who he or she truly is beyond their outside appearance. It is seeing the beauty inside someone's heart, where there is no makeup, clothing, or other modifiers to hide their true self. For me, the true definition of love is not seeing eye to eye but heart to heart.

♥ Love is doing good for others . . . doing what is in their best interest, not always what they think is best. God is the greatest example of love because he is love. Love is more than a feeling, it is action!

♥ Cherishing them for everything that they are . . . even their flaws.

♥ Love is hard to explain. It's a feeling. Love is feeling totally comfortable with someone and being able to express all your feelings to him or her. Love demands trust and honesty. Love is a connection between people which goes beyond need and want. Love is love.

♡♡♡♡♡♡♡♡♡♡♡♡♡♡♡♡♡

♥ Have you ever been afraid to fall in love?

_____

_____

_____

♥ If so, what were you afraid of?

_____

_____

_____

♥ Do you still feel this way?

_____

_____

_____

The Road to Love

The road to love is so dark.
Help me.
I'm frightened of a broken heart.
Protect me.
I fear I am all alone.
Stay with me.
I feel like I'm getting lost.
Guide me.
I need to know you're beside me.
Take my hand.
Should I just give up?
Encourage me.
I want to feel comfort.
Hold me.
I'm not sure if I have a purpose.
Need me.
Help me take down my brick wall.
Love me.

Lindsey Hartman

♥ Can you relate to this poem?

The more deeply you understand other people,
the more you will appreciate them,
the more reverent you will feel about them.
To touch the soul of another human being
is to walk on holy ground.

Stephen R. Covey

♥ What does this quote mean to you?

_____

_____

_____

_____

_____

_____

_____

_____

_____

♥ Do you think love is great or do you think love stinks?

_____

_____

_____

_____

_____

_____

_____

♥ Have you ever told anyone you loved him or her? If so, who said it first and how did it happen?

_____

_____

_____

_____

_____

_____

_____

♥ Have you ever sworn you would never fall in love again?

_____
_____
_____
_____
_____
_____
_____

♥ Did you?

_____
_____
_____
_____
_____
_____
_____

The following is a poem that was submitted to us. A young man who spoke of his great admiration for this girl sent it to us. He tells us in his letter that he has had a crush on her for four months and on this particular day he is sitting next to her in the library. He leans over and asks her to write a poem and the following is what she came up with in five minutes. (I'm impressed!)

How Odd a Feeling

How odd a feeling is this;
almost nothing
But yet it lays deep within
my chest and
gently pushes
itself out to
each fingertip.

How odd a feeling is this
that leaves me
wondering and wanting.
That leaves a
warmth
throughout me.

How odd a feeling is this
that causes my
world to shake
and the waters to flood.

How odd a feeling is this
that it burns deep
in my soul
so deep that it places
fire upon my lips,
and laughter in my eyes.

How odd a feeling is this
that I do not know
any word to describe
it other
than
. . . love.

Rikki Knies

♥ Have you ever been in love?

_____

♥ If yes, describe it:

_____

_____

_____

_____

_____

_____

_____

_____

_____

_____

_____

_____

_____

_____

_____

♥ Have you ever questioned whether or not what you were feeling was "TRUE LOVE"?

♥ Has anyone else ever told you, "You don't even know what love is"?

_____

_____

_____

_____

_____

_____

♥ How did that make you feel? Did you believe what they said?

_____

_____

_____

_____

_____

_____

_____

One doesn't fall into love,
one grows into love, and love grows in him.

Karl Menninger

♥ What do you think of this quote?

_____

_____

_____

_____

_____

_____

_____

_____

_____

_____

_____

_____

_____

♥ Do you believe there is one perfect person out there for you?

_____

♥ If so, list the qualities that person will possess:

1. _____

2. _____

3. _____

4. _____

5. _____

6. _____

7. _____

8. _____

9. _____

10. _____

♥ Would you rather have one long-lasting love or experience many loves throughout your life?

Love

Love is red like a rose
Love is green like the grass
Love is the moments you don't want to pass

Love is bright like the sun
Love is wet like the rain
Love is giving and losing and learning and pain

Love smells fresh like the flowers
It's blue as the sky
It's your smile when you laugh and your tears when you cry

Love is soft like a baby
It's rough like the sand
Love is the feeling of holding a hand

Love can't be bought
For no price is it sold
Love is the woman who's wrinkled and old

It's the chirp of the birds as they sing to the trees
It is sweet just like honey and sounds like the bees

Love is a teddy bear missing its eyes
Love comes in every shape, color and size

Love is the boy who just lost his first tooth
Love can grow old but it still keeps its youth

Love is the friend that you always will miss
Love's not uptight but a warm gentle kiss

Love is hot chocolate on a cold winter day
Love is the child that asked you to play

Love sings not solo but sings in a pair
Love is not selfish, it's something you share

Love is the sickness we all want to feel
Love is a Band-Aid that helps you to heal

Love is accepting and caring and kind
When you're not looking it's something you'll find

When your beauty is gone, you are wrinkled and old
You will always have love it can never be sold

When you grow old, and after you're gone
Your spirit will live through the love you've passed on.

Danielle Rosenblatt

♥ Write a poem or a quote about falling in love:

_____

_____

_____

_____

_____

_____

_____

_____

_____

_____

_____

_____

_____

_____

_____

_____

_____

_____

Best Friend's Page

♥ Have your best friend write his or her advice to you about falling in love:

_____

_____

_____

_____

_____

_____

♥ Have your best friend write his or her definition of love:

_____

_____

_____

_____

_____

_____

Colin's Pages

Falling in Love

Love is not a term that should be thrown around. Save it for times when you really mean it. Save it for someone who really deserves it.

Colin

Love is the strongest emotion that one person can feel for another person. Being "in love" is the end all/be all. It is the it of its. That is why it is so important to honor it and keep it sacred. That is why you don't want to tell someone "I love you" when that isn't really what is happening. It is easy to get caught up in the moment and want to tell your boyfriend/girlfriend "I love you," especially if you think that is what they want to hear.

Remember to say what you mean, not what you think someone wants to hear. Don't be in a hurry to say "I love you" if you are not sure. You will know when you are ready and you won't have to question whether or not it is love you are feeling.

I have another kind of challenge when it comes to love. I tend to close myself off from my emotions, especially if I think someone is getting too close. What I am now discovering is that it hurts much more to not be open to love. The lack of love or the inability to feel it is worse than the possibility of losing it someday. I am working at opening my heart and learning to trust because I don't want to miss out on this wonderful thing.

Colin

Colin's Questions

♥ What does "LOVE" mean to you and what do you reserve the words "I LOVE YOU" for?

_____

_____

_____

_____

♥ Are you ever frightened of love?

_____

_____

_____

_____

♥ When you get scared do you become distant and aloof?

_____

_____

_____

_____

♥ Write about ways in which you can open your heart more and become more trusting:

_____

_____

_____

_____

_____

_____

_____

_____

_____

_____

_____

_____

_____

_____

three

All These New Feelings

The heart has eyes which the
brain knows nothing of.

Charles Perkhurst

All These New Feelings

There is no way to know
before experiencing.

Dr. Robert Anthony

Without a doubt, the most difficult thing about becoming a teenager is all the new feelings that come with it. You go from living a pretty simple life to being bombarded with feelings you have never felt before. To make it even more difficult the same exact thing is happening to everyone you know.

Textbooks on adolescence talk about these new feelings as being very self-critical. I certainly remember having those feelings when I was a teen. Every little fault or imperfection became huge. If I had a pimple, for example, I was sure that everyone could see it and that everyone was looking at it. If I didn't know the answer to a question in class or if I made a social "blunder," the embarrassment was immense.

Try to remember as you experience these new feelings that that is all they are . . . feelings. They are not realities: Feelings are not facts. You may *feel* like everyone is judging you but quite honestly they are too busy worrying about themselves to even notice you most of the time. You may *feel* like no one loves you, but you have only closed your heart to yourself and it is because of that that you don't *feel* loved.

Please be kind to yourself and to others. Everyone you know is scared and insecure at one time or another. If you can show them kindness during these times, it will be easier to be kind to yourself when things get overwhelming. Try to let the feelings just pass on through, much like a wave. They come and they go.

♥ Make a list of "new feelings" you are experiencing:

For example:

I like boys/girls, I feel insecure around groups of people, I am uncomfortable around members of the opposite sex, etc.

1. _____

2. _____

3. _____

4. _____

5. _____

6. _____

7. _____

8. _____

9. _____

10. _____

♥ Make a list of the changes you see happening to your friends:

1. _____

2. _____

3. _____

4. _____

5. _____

6. _____

7. _____

8. _____

9. _____

10. _____

♥ Give an example of how "all these new feelings" are changing your life:

_____

_____

_____

_____

_____

_____

_____

_____

_____

_____

_____

_____

_____

_____

_____

_____

_____

_____

*M*any experts say that being a teenager means being extremely self-critical.

♥ Have you noticed that you are more critical of yourself now than you used to be?

_____

_____

_____

_____

_____

_____

♥ What kinds of things do you criticize about yourself?

_____

_____

_____

_____

_____

_____

♥ Are you overly critical of other people also?

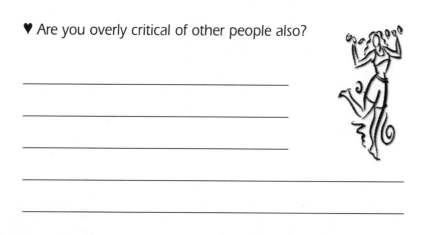

_____

_____

_____

_____

_____

_____

♥ If yes, list some of the things that drive you crazy in other people:

1. _____

2. _____

3. _____

4. _____

5. _____

6. _____

7. _____

8. _____

9. _____

10. _____

♥ What is your relationship with your parents like?

_____

_____

_____

_____

I? I? I? I? I? I? I? I? I? I? I? I? I? I?

♥ Write them a letter expressing all the new feelings you are having and how they affect your relationship with them. (It is up to you whether or not you give the letter to them.)

_____

_____

_____

_____

_____

_____

_____

_____

_____

_____

♥ How would you describe your parents' relationship with each other?

_____

_____

_____

_____

_____

_____

_____

_____

_____

_____

_____

_____

_____

_____

_____

♥ Ask your parents to write you a letter. The letter should be about the changes they see in you as you become a young adult.

_____

_____

_____

_____

_____

_____

_____

_____

_____

_____

_____

_____

_____

_____

♥ Imagine what you will be like in five years. Write about it:

_____

_____

_____

_____

_____

_____

_____

_____

_____

_____

_____

_____

_____

_____

_____

♥ When was the first time you realized you liked a boy/girl as more than just a friend?

_____

_____

_____

_____

_____

_____

_____

♥ How did you deal with it?

_____

_____

_____

_____

_____

_____

_____

♥ Make a list of things about yourself that are new and different:

♥ What is the most difficult thing about being a teenager?

_____

_____

_____

_____

_____

_____

_____

♥ What is the best thing about being a teenager?

_____

_____

_____

_____

_____

_____

_____

We must adjust to changing times and
still hold true to unchanging
principles.

Julia Coleman

Even though things are rapidly changing for you right now, it is important to have values and principles that do not change.

♥ Make a list of the values and principles you will stand by no matter what:

1. _____

2. _____

3. _____

4. _____

5. _____

6. _____

7. _____

8. _____

9. _____

10. _____

Best Friend's Page

♥ Have your best friend make a list of the changes he or she sees happening in you:

1. _____

2. _____

3. _____

4. _____

5. _____

6. _____

7. _____

8. _____

9. _____

10. _____

Colin's Pages

All These New Feelings

With all these new feelings and all the confusions that teenagers face we really need a strong support system. Friends are just that, and they are there for the long haul. Try your best to be a good and loyal friend and to not turn your back on your friends when they need you. It is really important to remember not to put boyfriends or girlfriends ahead of friendships.

I am lucky because I have two friends whom I consider to be the best. In fact, you may know who they are from *The Real World/Road Rules Casting Special*. Trevor and Mike have been there for me through many things—both good and bad. My friends are what made it possible for me to enjoy high school. I always felt secure that they would be there for me when I needed them. We had other friends who blew us off for a girlfriend or boyfriend, and, to be honest, when they realized they had messed up, it was too late.

If there is one message I want to pass on to you, it is to cherish your friends and never toss them aside for a girlfriend, boyfriend or anything else that might come along. Cherish them for the gifts they are.

Colin

Colin's Questions

♥ Have you ever treated a friend poorly in order to do something you felt was more important? Describe what happened. Was it worth it?

_____

_____

_____

_____

_____

_____

_____

_____

_____

_____

_____

_____

_____

_____

♥ I think it's important from time to time to do an inventory of friends! Take these lines below to list five friends whom you appreciate. After each name include a brief reason why you appreciate him or her:

1. _____

_____

_____

2. _____

_____

_____

3. _____

_____

_____

4. _____

_____

_____

5. _____

_____

_____

_____

_____

♥ Take these next lines to list the names of five friends you have or have had in your life who don't or didn't treat you right. After each name briefly describe how that person's actions have made you feel and what you would like to tell him or her:

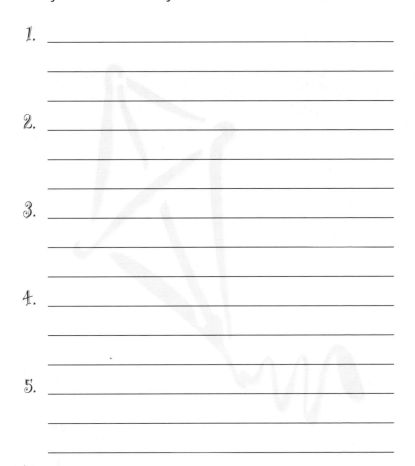

1. _____

_____

_____

2. _____

_____

_____

3. _____

_____

_____

4. _____

_____

_____

5. _____

_____

_____

The key to this exercise is to learn to tell the people who don't treat us right how their actions make us feel. It may become necessary to detach yourself from these people if they are not treating you how you deserve to be treated.

four

There Is a First Time for Everything

We always believe our first love to be our
last and our last to be our first.

George John Whyte-Melville

There Is a First Time for Everything

Most of us will never forget the first time we fell in love or the first time we were kissed. Whether you have experienced your first love or are just dreaming about the day when it will happen, remember that these are precious times—treat them with special care. Don't rush things and don't set your expectations too high. If you remember these two things, you will get through it with a lot more ease and a lot more joy.

No one has ever loved anyone the way everyone wants to be loved.

Mignon McLaughlin

♥ Do you remember the first time you had a crush on someone?

_____

_____

_____

_____

_____

_____

_____

♥ Write about it:

_____

_____

_____

_____

_____

_____

_____

♥ Describe your very first date:

_____

_____

_____

_____

_____

_____

_____

_____

_____

_____

_____

_____

_____

_____

_____

_____

♥ Describe your first boyfriend or girlfriend:

♥ If you're no longer together, how did it end?

No
Complaints

Why you like to kiss me so
I don't think I will ever know

But I will not complain right now
I'd rather kiss and wonder how

From night's last dusk to early dawn
We'll kiss and kiss until you're gone.

Christina Atkinson

♥ Have you ever been kissed? If so, describe it:

I can forget my very existence
in a deep kiss of you.

Byron Caldwell Smith

I find as I grow older that
I love those most whom I loved first.

Thomas Jefferson

♥ Do you think you will feel this way about your first love?

_____

_____

_____

_____

_____

_____

_____

_____

_____

_____

_____

_____

Best Friend's Pages

♥ Have your best friend write about the way you acted when you experienced your first crush:

_____

_____

_____

_____

_____

_____

♥ Your first date:

_____

_____

_____

_____

_____

_____

♥ Your first kiss:

_____

_____

_____

_____

_____

♥ Your first boyfriend or *girlfriend*:

_____

_____

_____

_____

_____

♥ Your first breakup:

_____

_____

_____

_____

_____

First Time for Everything

I think the difference between me and other people is that most people are "searching for love," whereas I think I am searching for "the ability to love." It is okay to be confused about what love is. How are you supposed to know what a certain feeling is if you have never felt it before? I'm nineteen and I have yet to be "in love" with anyone. I can't even say that I know what love is!

I can say that I have *loved* someone, but in my mind there is a difference between "loving" someone and "being in love" with someone. I already have a difficult time expressing my feelings. I am in no hurry to profess my love to someone whom I may later find out I don't love. There is a pleasant mystery to looking forward to finding that person who is going to challenge and complete me in every way.

It is important not to rush any stage of your life. Enjoy the present, enjoy the mystery involved in waiting to experience your "firsts." Enjoy the questions and the confusion. In other words, enjoy your innocence because when it is gone you will long for it. And remember that you are not alone: I'm nineteen and I still have no idea what love is!

Colin

Colin's Questions

♥ What does love mean to you?

_____

_____

_____

_____

♥ Do you think there is a difference between "loving" someone and "being in love" with someone?

_____

_____

_____

_____

♥ What do you think is the difference between "liking" and "loving" someone?

_____

_____

_____

_____

♥ Can you draw a distinction between loving family, loving friends and loving boyfriends or girlfriends? If so, what are the differences?

♡♡♡♡♡♡♡♡♡♡♡♡♡♡♡♡♡

_____

_____

_____

_____

♡♡♡♡♡♡♡♡♡♡♡♡♡♡♡♡♡

_____

_____

_____

_____

♡♡♡♡♡♡♡♡♡♡♡♡♡♡♡♡♡

_____

_____

_____

_____

five

Do You Like Me?

Remember one thing only: that it's you—
nobody else—who determines your destiny and
decides your fate. Nobody else can be alive for you;
nor can you be alive for anybody else.

e. e. cummings

Do You Like Me?

One of the scariest things we can ever do is to put our feelings out there, not knowing if they will be returned. It is a brave soul who tells another of his or her feelings for that person, or happens to mention it to their best friend, if they do not know how that person feels in return.

There are thousands of stories of people who never have the courage to take this chance, but in every case, it is something they live to regret.

If you like someone, be proud of it. It means that your heart is open and you are able to see beauty and goodness in another person. This, by itself, is a good thing. You could not feel this way if you did not see these same things in yourself.

At the same time, remember if that person does not feel the same way, it does not mean you are unworthy of their love. It is just one of life's mysteries. Sometimes love is mutual and sometimes it is not.

♥ How do you know when a guy or girl likes you?

_____

_____

_____

_____

_____

_____

_____

_____

_____

_____

_____

_____

_____

_____

_____

♥ What do you do when you like someone? Do you tell that person?

_____

_____

_____

_____

_____

_____

_____

_____

_____

_____

_____

_____

_____

_____

♥ Have you ever had a crush on someone you considered "out of your league"?

_____

_____

_____

_____

_____

_____

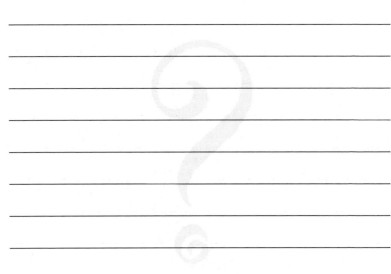

♥ What happened?

_____

_____

_____

_____

_____

_____

_____

What qualities do you find most attractive in members of the opposite sex?

♥ What are some things guys like about girls?

_____

_____

_____

_____

_____

_____

_____

_____

♥ _____   ♥ _____

♥ _____   ♥ _____

♥ _____   ♥ _____

♥ _____   ♥ _____

♥ _____   ♥ _____

♥ _____   ♥ _____

♥ _____   ♥ _____

♥ _____   ♥ _____

♥ _____   ♥ _____

♥ _____   ♥ _____

♥ _____   ♥ _____

♥ What are some things girls like about guys?

_____

_____

_____

_____

_____

_____

_____

♥ _____   ♥ _____

♥ _____   ♥ _____

♥ _____   ♥ _____

♥ _____   ♥ _____

♥ _____   ♥ _____

♥ _____   ♥ _____

♥ _____   ♥ _____

♥ _____   ♥ _____

♥ _____   ♥ _____

♥ _____   ♥ _____

♥ _____   ♥ _____

Behold the turtle. He makes progress
only when he sticks his neck out.

James Conant

♥ Is there someone you like who doesn't know about your feelings?

♥ If so, write them a letter and tell them how you feel. (You do not have to give it to them, just write it either way. It will help you to understand how you feel.)

♥ Have you ever done anything embarrassing in front of a guy or girl you liked?

_____

_____

_____

_____

_____

_____

_____

_____

_____

_____

_____

_____

_____

_____

_____

True love comes quietly, without banners
or flashing lights. If you hear bells,
get your ears checked.

Erich Segal

♥ What does this quote mean to you?

66 ──────────────────────────────

────────────────────────────────────

────────────────────────────────────

────────────────────────────────────

────────────────────────────────────

────────────────────────────────────

────────────────────────────────────

────────────────────────────────────

────────────────────────────────────

───────────────────────────── 99

Best Friend's Pages

♥ Have your best friend write about what he or she thinks are the qualities the opposite sex likes in you:

♥ _____

♥ _____

♥ _____

♥ _____

♥ _____

♥ _____

♥ _____   ♥ _____

♥ _____   ♥ _____

♥ _____   ♥ _____

♥ _____   ♥ _____

♥ _____   ♥ _____

♥ _____   ♥ _____

♥ _____   ♥ _____

♥ _____   ♥ _____

♥ _____   ♥ _____

♥ _____   ♥ _____

♥ Have your best friend make a list of the qualities he or she thinks you like in the opposite sex:

Colin's Pages

Do You Like Me?

If you ask someone out and they say no, think of it as his or her loss. That person will be missing out on getting to know a great person. This will lead you to have confidence in yourself . . . and, believe it or not, both women and men are attracted to confidence. Note: I said "confidence," not "arrogance." Nobody likes people who are full of themselves.

Colin

Courage is not the lack of fear, but acting in spite of it.

Mark Twain

It is extremely hard to put yourself out on the line and ask someone out. I still have trouble with this one. I just don't like making myself susceptible to being rejected. My dad once told me that it took him until his thirties to be able to approach a woman he wanted to ask out and "not care" whether he was rejected or not. I try to remind myself that it is always better to know if someone feels the same way than to be left in the dark. If it turns out the person is not interested in you, be easy on yourself and understand that it may be that the two of you were not meant for each other. Not all people are meant to be together.

Colin

Colin's Question

♥ What would be the worst thing that could happen when you tell someone you like him or her or ask someone out?

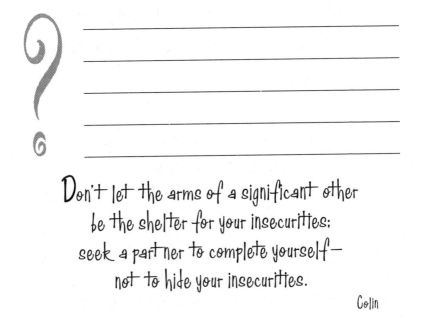

Don't let the arms of a significant other
be the shelter for your insecurities;
seek a partner to complete yourself—
not to hide your insecurities.

Colin

*I*f you like somebody, make sure you like them for the right reasons. We all search for somebody who is going to make us more secure and help us grow as a person in many ways. Your partner should not be there to pick up the slack where you are weak, but to help you to become strong in those areas. He or she should help you to grow, not mask your insecurities.

♥ What are some areas you would like to improve in yourself?

♥ How might a boyfriend or girlfriend help you to develop and grow in these areas?

six

When Friends Become More

Friendship is constant in all other things,
except in the office and
affairs of love.

William Shakespeare

Love is only chatter.
Friends are all that matter.

Gillett Burgess

When Friends Become More

Talk about complicated. It doesn't get more complicated than this. You and your best friend have been hanging out since third grade. You know each other's deepest secrets and biggest insecurities. One day you look at him (or her) and you see someone completely different. He or she is a total hottie. Now what?

Poetry and books, plays and movies have been written about this wonderfully mixed-up mess. Now it's your turn.

♥ Make a list of all your friends of the opposite sex:

♡ ✩   1. _____

♡ ✩   2. _____

♡ ✩   3. _____

♡ ✩   4. _____

♡ ✩   5. _____

♡ ✩   6. _____

♡ ✩   7. _____

♡ ✩   8. _____

♡ ✩   9. _____

♡ ✩   10. _____

♥ Now go over the list and put a red heart next to anyone's name whom you could feel more than friendship for. Put a blue star next to the names of ones who may have feelings for you. Are there any names without a heart or star next to them? Maybe one or two, maybe not.

*M*any people believe there is no such thing as an innocent friendship between members of the opposite sex.

♥ What do you think?

_____

_____

_____

_____

_____

_____

_____

_____

_____

_____

_____

_____

_____

_____

_____

_____

♥ Have you ever developed a crush on a friend of yours?

♥ What happened? How did you handle it?

♥ Has a friend ever had a crush on you?

_____

_____

_____

_____

♥ How did you know?

_____

_____

_____

_____

♥ And how did you handle it? Was it mutual?

_____

_____

_____

_____

♥ Do you have any friends right now whom you could see being in a relationship with someday? Who?

_____

_____

_____

_____

_____

_____

_____

_____

♥ Have you ever had a crush on your friend's boyfriend or girl-friend? What happened?

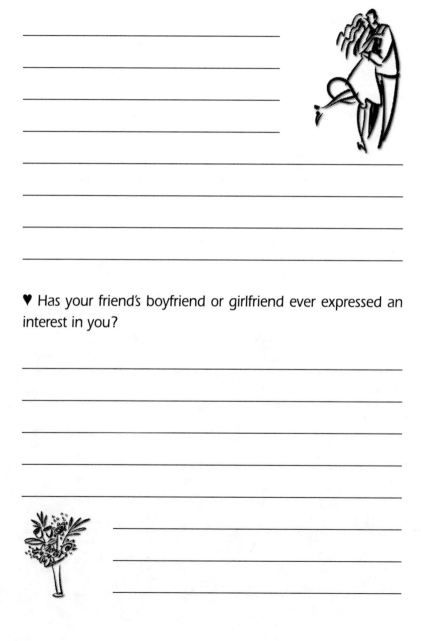

_____

_____

_____

_____

_____

_____

_____

_____

♥ Has your friend's boyfriend or girlfriend ever expressed an interest in you?

_____

_____

_____

_____

_____

_____

_____

_____

♥ Did you ever fall in love with a close friend?

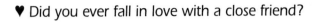

_____

_____

_____

_____

_____

_____

_____

_____

_____

_____

_____

_____

_____

_____

_____

_____

_____

_____

♥ Have you ever developed a close friendship with somebody on whom you had a crush?

_____

_____

_____

_____

_____

_____

♥ Did you become that person's friend just to get closer to him or her?

_____

_____

_____

_____

♥ What was the outcome?

_____

_____

_____

_____

♥ If you have a crush on one of your friends, what would be
the ideal outcome?

_____

_____

_____

_____

_____

_____

_____

_____

_____

_____

_____

_____

_____

♥ What is the best way to let a friend know you have feelings for him or her?

_____

_____

_____

_____

_____

_____

_____

_____

_____

_____

♥ Have you ever gotten into a relationship with a friend of yours only to later regret it? If so, what happened?

_____

_____

_____

_____

_____

_____

_____

♥ Are you friends again?

_____

_____

_____

_____

_____

_____

_____

_____

♥ Have you and a friend of yours ever liked the same person?

_____

_____

_____

_____

_____

_____

♥ How did you two handle it?

_____

_____

_____

_____

_____

_____

_____

_____

_____

_____

Best Friend's Page

♥ Have your best friend answer the following questions about you:

♥ Do you know of anyone right now who may have feelings for your best friend?

_____

_____

_____

♥ Is there anyone that your best friend would make a cute couple with?

_____

_____

_____

♥ Have you ever liked the same guy or girl? If so, what happened?

_____

_____

_____

Colin's Pages

When Friends Become More

I, as well as friends of mine, have developed crushes on good friends. Keep in mind that friends are extremely precious and you should always be mindful of their feelings. If you develop feelings for a friend of yours, let him or her know. Much like asking somebody out, you will never know if mutual feelings exist unless you put your feelings out there.

If you find yourself on the other side of this potentially awkward scenario, be honest and be considerate. If your feelings are not as strong as your friend's, let him or her down easily. Be sensitive—in all likelihood, your friend has had these feelings bottled up for a long time.

I had a huge crush on one of my friends in high school. She didn't feel the same way and instead of letting me know she wasn't interested, she avoided the issue. Unfortunately, this bred a lingering feeling of "possibility" in my mind. It would have hurt a lot less if she had been forthright, honest and sensitive.

Sometimes you can get involved with a friend only to have the relationship not work out. Things *can* go back to the way they were before you two became involved. I have become involved with friends of mine in the past and even though the relationship didn't work out, we were able to go back to our close friendship. We just realized we weren't right for each other and we were better off as friends. We remain close to this day.

Colin

Colin's Questions

♥ What is more important to you: a boyfriend or girlfriend, or a friendship?

☐ Boyfriend   ☐ Girlfriend   ☐ Friend

♥ If you were to fall in love with a friend of yours, would you tell that person? If so, how would you let that person know about your feelings?

_____

_____

_____

_____

_____

_____

_____

_____

_____

seven

Unrequited Love

Life is not the way it is supposed to be.
It's the way it is. The way you deal with it is
what makes the difference.

Virginia Satir

Unrequited Love

Unrequited love is one of life's more painful experiences. It feels like you are pouring your heart out to someone and they are letting it fall to the ground, unrecognized and, even worse, unreturned. It feels like we might not survive if we do not receive the love back. Every terrible thing we have ever felt or thought about ourselves comes to the surface and makes us feel totally unlovable. There are two very important things to remember when it comes to unrequited love:

♥ If someone doesn't return your love it doesn't mean you're unlovable.

♥ Be kind if you ever find yourself in a position in which you are unable to return someone's love.

Aside from these two things, remember it will pass, and you will heal. Be kind to yourself.

Your Game

The dice are rolled, the wheel spins
My turn has come, your game begins.

I move my piece across the board.
I skip a turn, and you have scored.

To get ahead is my one goal,
Yet "go back two" is what I roll.

And so I'm back where I have started
Empty-handed, broken-hearted.

I try again, I need to win,
Still you resist to let me in.

You make the rules, and break them, too,
And I do not know what to do.

When I catch up and it's a tie,
You roll a double and pass me by.

Sometimes I think you'll let me win,
But that is when the lies begin.

The way you cheat at your own game
Leaves nothing for you but the blame.

Over and over I seem to lose;
To play again I always choose.

And foolishly I still pretend
That soon your stupid game will end.

Rebecca Scida

♥ Have you ever loved someone who didn't love you back?

_____

_____

_____

_____

_____

_____

♥ Describe what it was like and how you dealt with it:

_____

_____

_____

_____

_____

_____

_____

_____

_____

♥ If your very best friend was in love with someone who did not return that love, what would be your advice to her or him?

_____

_____

_____

_____

_____

_____

_____

_____

_____

_____

_____

_____

_____

_____

_____

_____

♥ Have you ever been unable to return someone's love or affection for you?

♥ Draw a picture of yourself or write a poem expressing what you feel like when you're feeling unlovable:

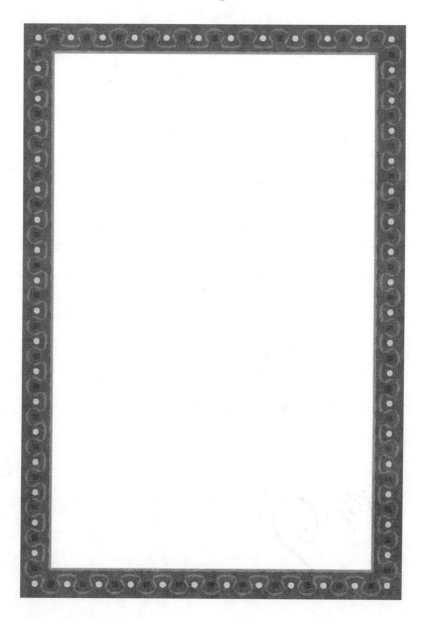

The heart has its reasons, which
reason does not know.

Blaise Pascal

♥ What does this quote mean to you?

_____

_____

_____

_____

_____

_____

_____

_____

_____

_____

_____

_____

_____

♥ Have you ever loved someone from afar?

_____

_____

_____

_____

I? I? I? I? I? I? I? I? I? I? I? I? I? I?

♥ If so, did you let them know you loved them?

_____

_____

_____

_____

_____

_____

_____

_____

_____

_____

_____

♥ Do you believe in love at first sight?

_____

_____

_____

_____

_____

_____

_____

♥ Has it ever happened to you?

_____

_____

_____

_____

_____

_____

_____

♥ Write about the lessons you have learned from "unrequited love":

Best Friend's Page

♥ Have your best friend write about his or her experience with unrequited love. (Best friend: Make sure to include what you learned from the experience.):

_____

_____

_____

_____

_____

_____

_____

_____

_____

_____

_____

_____

_____

Colin's Pages

Unrequited Love

*L*ove means different things to different people. We feel it in different ways and at different times. It is a precarious situation when one person feels they are "in love" and the other doesn't.

One night my girlfriend (at the time) told me she "loved me" on the phone. An awkward silence followed. I didn't know what to say. I wanted to be both true to myself and sensitive to her feelings at the same time. Unfortunately, I couldn't say what I didn't feel. The awkward silence on my end of the line that day put a strain on both our hearts and our relationship from that day forward.

I really admired her for having the courage to be vulnerable and say what she felt. However, I didn't say, "I love you" that day because I want to be able to mean it when I say it. There is a great deal of integrity in being true to your heart. It is important to realize that love doesn't have to be mutual. Although it hurts when it's not, know that just because the person you love does not love you the same way in return doesn't mean that person doesn't care for you deeply.

Colin

Colin's Questions

♥ If you had strong feelings for someone who didn't feel the same way, what would be the best way for that person to handle it?

_____

_____

_____

_____

_____

_____

_____

_____

_____

_____

_____

_____

eight

Now That We're Together

Love is an attempt to change a piece
of the dream world into reality.

Theodor Reik

Now That We're Together

We dream of the day we have a boyfriend or girlfriend as being the day when we will truly be happy. Although there are many happy times in a relationship, there are also problems: jealousy, insecurities, disagreements and different expectations. You may think, for instance, that now that you are in a relationship there will always be someone to be with on Friday nights. However, your partner may inform you that Friday nights have long been reserved for friends, and he or she has no intention of changing that.

Once again, if you remember that this is a learning experience and all difficulties can lead to a better understanding of love, then you will be okay. Try not to let the hard times take over the good ones and remember to keep your sense of humor.

Use these pages to vent your feelings before unloading them on your partner. Also, use these pages to gain perspective and a better understanding.

The Way You . . .

The way you look at me when I am talking lets me know
you really care, that you really are listening.

The way you touch me, ever so gently, makes me know
you will never hurt me.

The way you speak into my eyes and listen for
my opinion lets me know you value me.

The way you let me be myself makes me know
that you aren't judging me.

The way you introduce me to your friends and family
lets me know you are not ashamed of me.

The way you act around me makes me know that you
are comfortable and are not putting on an act.

The way you do not rush me lets me know
that you respect me and value me.

The way you make time for me makes me feel
special and important.

The way you smile at me lets me know that
you are only thinking of me.

The way you don't get mad at me makes me know
you will always be patient with me.

The way you think of me as your friend lets me know
I am more than just your girlfriend.

The way you treat me lets me know that I am very lucky
to be loved by someone as special as you.

Kristen Keys

♥ If you are in a relationship, describe what it is like:

_____

_____

_____

_____

_____

_____

_____

_____

_____

_____

_____

                           _____

                           _____

                           _____

                           _____

                           _____

                           _____

♥ If you are not currently in a relationship, describe what you want in a relationship:

_____

_____

_____

_____

_____

_____

_____

_____

_____

_____

_____

_____

_____

♥ What is the sweetest thing your boyfriend or girlfriend has ever said to you?

_____

_____

_____

_____

_____

_____

_____

♥ What is the sweetest thing your boyfriend or girlfriend has ever done for you?

_____

_____

_____

_____

_____

_____

_____

Be to her virtues very kind
Be to her faults a little blind.

Mathew Prior

♥ What does this quote mean to you?

66

99

♡ ♡ ♡ ♡ ♡ ♡ ♡ ♡ ♡ ♡ ♡ ♡ ♡ ♡

We posted a question on our Web site *http://www.teenagechickensoup.com* asking boys and girls, "What do you look for in a boyfriend/ girlfriend?"

The following is a list of some of their answers:

♥ A guy who doesn't make me explain why I am grumpy (when I am) but instead just holds me until I am ready to discuss it.

♥ I look for someone with a sense of humor.

♥ I want someone I can trust. *(This was the most common response from both girls and guys.)*

♥ I want a guy who isn't afraid to say what he is feeling.

♥ I like it when a girl laughs at my jokes and understands my feelings.

♥ I look for a person who will be able to be my friend no matter what happens between us—whether we stay together or not.

♥ I look for honesty and sincerity. I also like girls who smile a lot.

♥ I look for someone who will love me for who I am.

♡ ♡ ♡ ♡ ♡ ♡ ♡ ♡ ♡ ♡ ♡ ♡ ♡ ♡

♥ What is your favorite feature of your boyfriend or girlfriend?

_____

_____

_____

_____

_____

_____

_____

♥ Is there anything you dislike about your boyfriend or girlfriend?

_____

_____

_____

_____

_____

_____

_____

♥ How did you meet your boyfriend or girlfriend?

_____

_____

_____

_____

_____

_____

_____

_____

_____

_____

_____

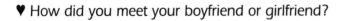

_____

_____

_____

_____

_____

Love is an act of endless forgiveness,
a tender look which becomes a habit.

Peter Ustinov

♥ Have you ever gotten into an argument with your boyfriend or girlfriend? If so, what was it over? How was it resolved?

_____

_____

_____

_____

_____

_____

_____

_____

_____

_____

_____

_____

_____

♥ Do you and your boyfriend or girlfriend have a song? If so, what is it?

_____

_____

♥ What song makes you think of your boyfriend or girlfriend?

_____

_____

♥ What movie reminds you most of your relationship?

_____

_____

♥ If you were to cast the movie of your life story, who would play you? Why?

_____

_____

_____

_____

♥ Who would play your boyfriend or girlfriend?

_____

_____

♥ List things that the two of you have in common:

1. _____
2. _____
3. _____
4. _____
5. _____
6. _____
7. _____
8. _____
9. _____
10. _____

♥ List the areas in which the two of you are complete opposites:

1. _____

2. _____

3. _____

4. _____

5. _____

6. _____

7. _____

8. _____

9. _____

10. _____

♥ What is your favorite memory regarding your relationship?

♥ What are your secrets for making a relationship last?

_____

_____

_____

_____

_____

_____

_____

_____

♥ What is the longest relationship you have ever been in?

_____

_____

_____

_____

_____

_____

_____

Without trust you'll never be free
to love and be loved.

Pat Feinman

♥ What does this quote mean to you?

66 _____

_____

_____

_____ 99

♥ Have you ever been jealous? ☐ Yes ☐ No

♥ How did you handle it?

_____

_____

_____

_____

♥ Do you trust your boyfriend or girlfriend? ☐ Yes ☐ No

♥ Do you think you have difficulty trusting? ☐ Yes ☐ No

♥ Do your parents like your girlfriend or boyfriend?

_____

_____

_____

_____

♥ Why or why not?

_____

_____

_____

_____

_____

_____

_____

_____

_____

♥ Have you ever had a cyber boyfriend or girlfriend?

□ Yes   □ No

♥ If so, what happened?

_____

_____

_____

_____

_____

_____

_____

_____

_____

_____

_____

_____

_____

♥ Is there something you wish you could have said to the person you were last in a relationship with? If so, write it here:

Best Friend's Page

♥ Have your best friend answer the following questions about the relationship you are in or the one you were in most recently:

♥ What is a song lyric that reminds you of your friend and his or her boyfriend or girlfriend?

_____

_____

_____

♥ What movie reminds you of their relationship?

_____

_____

_____

♥ Do you think that your friend is being treated as well as he or she deserves? Why or why not?

_____

_____

_____

Colin's Pages

Now That We're Together

Relationships are not all smooth sailing.
There are always difficult areas,
things you must work through
and struggle to understand.

Colin

*M*any people enjoy the challenge of chasing after someone but lose interest once feelings become mutual. The real challenge is growing *with* someone, not simply "catching" them. Pursue somebody because you want to be with that person, not because it is a challenge for your ego.

Once in a relationship, I have found it challenging to maintain the balance between being a good friend to my guy friends and spending time with my girlfriend. Sometimes being around the two at the same time is especially tough. It's difficult to show a sensitive side around guy friends without being ridiculed and teased. Guys can be pretty harsh with each other, especially during adolescence. Ideally, friends would encourage all aspects of ourselves; in reality, this is not always the case. Mostly, guys tease each other about relationships because they are jealous of the time and energy spent with the girlfriend. They miss spending quality time with their close friend. I have learned that it is futile to try to please or impress my guy friends by treating my girlfriend differently around them. I just act how I want to act with my girlfriend and let my friends accept this other side of me.

At the same time, I have also learned how important it is not to neglect your friends once you are in a relationship. Your friends will be around when your relationship ends. Every group of friends has that one person who "disappears" when they begin a relationship. You don't hear from them for like a year and you know why. Don't be that person! Friendships provide a lifetime of love and understanding; most relationships are fleeting.

Colin

Colin's Questions

♥ Have you ever experienced difficulty maintaining balance between a boyfriend or girlfriend and your friends?

_____

_____

_____

_____

_____

♥ How have you experienced growing _with_ a partner?

_____

_____

_____

_____

_____

_____

nine

Breaking Up Is Hard to Do

The real genius for love lies not in getting into, but getting out of, love.

George Moore

Breaking Up Is Hard to Do

You must live through the time
when everything hurts.

Stephen Spender

When a relationship ends it is like a mini-death. No matter what the circumstance was that determined its conclusion, the pain is intense. It is important to grieve the end of a relationship and to understand that even if its end is for the best, it is still a sorrow-filled time.

As time passes you will heal, but to ensure a full healing you must allow yourself to feel the pain of the loss. Acknowledge your feelings by writing about them, talking with your friends about them or just simply letting yourself cry.

The love of parents and friends will help get you through it, and in time you will be stronger and wiser and ready to love again.

♥ Describe how your first relationship ended:

I
O

_____
_____
_____
_____
_____
_____
_____

♥ In looking back, were there any warning signs that the breakup was coming?

_____
_____
_____
_____
_____
_____
_____

♥ How did you heal or comfort yourself?

_____

_____

_____

_____

_____

_____

_____

_____

_____

_____

_____

_____

_____

_____

♥ If you left him or her, what did you say?

_____

_____

_____

_____

_____

♥ If he or she left you, what was your response?

_____

_____

_____

_____

♥ Are you friends now?

_____

_____

_____

_____

♥ If you have experienced more than one breakup, have you noticed anything similar about the breakups?

_____

_____

_____

_____

_____

_____

_____

_____

_____

_____

_____

_____

_____

_____

_____

_____

♥ Do you give yourself time to heal or do you move on to another relationship quickly?

_____

_____

_____

_____

_____

_____

_____

_____

_____

_____

_____

_____

_____

_____

_____

_____

♥ How have your close friends helped you through a breakup?

♥ Have you ever lost someone over something you wish you hadn't said or done? If so, what do you wish you could have done differently?

_____

_____

_____

_____

_____

_____

_____

_____

_____

_____

_____

_____

_____

♥ What is the best way to break up with someone?

♥ Have you ever reunited with someone after you had been broken up? If so, what was it like? Was it better or worse after you got back together?

A Heart Too Soft

The pain is within me I can't get it out.
It does me no good to scream and to shout.
The moans I emit and the tears that fall
Do nothing to ease my pain at all.

They say time's a healer. I pray that it's true.
And wait for the healing is all I can do.
For my heart has been broken, my faith in man crushed.
I trusted in others and in the end lost.

I've been such a fool, for too soft is my heart
And it opens wide up for each fiery dart.
What good is a heart that is tender and meek,
That smashes to pieces beneath others' feet?

Of what use can it be when it fills up with pain
For it trusts and it loves again and again.
A heart that is hard, that loves not at all,
That never will trust, feels no pain at all.

But it also feels nothing of life that is sweet.
Can it be there's a middle where hard and soft meet?
Should I go on believing in my fellow man?
Is it worth the great risk if I'm let down again?

In my soul I believe that the answer is yes,
For to live without love could never be best.
To never know friendship, what good would life be?
So the risks are worth taking, at least for me.

I'll guard my heart the best that I can,
Knowing that I'll get hurt again.
That's the risk I must take, and that's what I'll do,
For to live without love just never would do.

Nellie McDowell

Best Friend's Pages

♥ Have your best friend answer the following questions about you:

♥ If your best friend has experienced a breakup since you've been friends, describe how he or she seemed to handle it.

_____

_____

_____

_____

_____

_____

♥ Did you learn any coping skills from witnessing them go through the experience?

_____

_____

_____

_____

_____

♥ If you have experienced the breakup of a relationship, how did your best friend help you to cope?

_____

_____

_____

_____

_____

_____

_____

_____

_____

_____

_____

_____

_____

_____

_____

_____

Colin's Pages

Breaking Up Is Hard to Do

When you know it is time for a relationship to end it's best just to end it. The longer you wait, the messier things get.

Colin

For me, breaking up with someone is one of the most difficult things to do. The most difficult part is being able to say what you mean. If you did say exactly what was on your mind, it would come out sounding like this: "You're clingy, way too needy, you don't let me spend time with my friends, you like me way more than I like you, I never meant for it to get this serious." Or worse yet: "I like your best friend, you walk funny and your laugh is annoying!"

To avoid completely crushing the other person, men and women have developed a code language for breaking up. For example, Cindy wants to break up with Mark:

Cindy says: "I think you are really sweet, but I don't see us working out as anything but friends."

Cindy means: "I'm way too smart for you, I'm tired of your football stories and you have bad breath."

I think it is important these days to develop your own unique code or else the other person will know you're lying. For instance, you can no longer use the old "It's not you, it's *me*." This one doesn't work for a couple of reasons. First, it has been so overused that it has become a cliché. Second, of *course* it's them, that's why you're giving them the boot!

In all seriousness, try to be as honest and gentle as possible when breaking up with someone. Try to point to a certain problem in the relationship and use that to explain the reason it is not working out for you. If it's true, let them know that you would still like to maintain a friendship. If it's not true, don't lie; tell them you don't think it's healthy for you to be friends. Whenever possible, try your best to respect the other person's dignity by being sensitive and honest.

Colin

Colin's Questions

♥ I can't decide which is worse: breaking up with someone or being broken up with . . . what do you think?

_____

_____

_____

_____

_____

♥ If you were going to be "left" how would you want it to go down? What should he or she say?

_____

_____

_____

_____

_____

_____

♥ How should he or she act?

_____

_____

_____

_____

_____

_____

_____

♥ How would *you* do it?

_____

_____

_____

_____

_____

_____

_____

ten

Starting ☆ Over

'Tis hard to drop at once
old-standing love.

Catullus

Starting Over

You loved, you lost and you swore you were finished with love. But now that you have had some time to heal and learn, you are able to open your heart again and, who knows, maybe even fall in love.

Each time you go through heartache and come out on the other side you become stronger and more trusting of love. You begin to see that *even though there were pain-filled times, there were also some wonderful ones, too.* And you see that you are a better person for having allowed yourself to experience love and all that goes with it.

♥ Are you currently recovering from the loss of a love?

_____

_____

_____

_____

_____

_____

♥ If so, describe what you are feeling:

_____

_____

_____

_____

♥ Describe what your experience was after the end of your first relationship:

_____

_____

_____

_____

_____

_____

_____

_____

_____

_____

_____

_____

_____

_____

_____

_____

♥ Write about the things that helped you to heal:

♥ Make a list of things that you would recommend a friend do if they were suffering from the loss of a love:

1. _____

2. _____

3. _____

4. _____

5. _____

6. _____

7. _____

8. _____

9. _____

10. _____

♥ Have you ever sworn you would never fall in love again?

_____

_____

_____

_____

_____

_____

_____

♥ Do you still feel this way?

_____

_____

_____

_____

_____

_____

♥ Write a story or a poem about a person with a broken heart and their journey back to themselves:

_____

_____

_____

_____

_____

_____

_____

_____

_____

_____

_____

_____

_____

_____

_____

_____

Best Friend's Pages

♥ Have your best friend answer the following questions about you:

♥ When have you been most proud of your best friend in regards to a relationship or the breakup of a relationship?

_____

_____

_____

_____

_____

♥ What have you learned from your best friend regarding relationships?

_____

_____

_____

_____

_____

♥ Which one of the two of you is more sentimental?

_____

_____

_____

_____

_____

_____

_____

♥ Describe a time when your best friend helped you get over the loss of a love:

_____

_____

_____

_____

_____

_____

_____

_____

Starting Over

It's better to open your heart after having lost love than to close off your emotions.

Colin

Starting over means the possibility of love is once again in the air. It gives you a chance to meet someone new; a chance to develop a crush; a chance to get that tingly feeling that runs through your body when you kiss someone that you like for the first time; a chance to get nervous before the first phone call, the first date or the first kiss; a chance to look in the person's direction and wonder if he or she is looking in yours; a chance to exchange glances, smiles, names or phone numbers; a chance to notice his or her smell and touch. But, most of all, starting over gives you a chance to get back in the game! Oh yeah, the chase is on!

Whatever you do, don't close your heart to others. I've done this for most of my life and am just now learning how to let people in. Ironically, in trying to keep myself from getting hurt, I ended up depriving myself of things that I really needed and wanted. Open your heart!

Colin

Colin's Questions

♥ Relationships . . . are they worth it?

_____

_____

_____

_____

_____

_____

_____

♥ What is the best remedy for healing a broken heart?

_____

_____

_____

_____

_____

_____

_____

♥ Do you feel open to love?

_____

_____

_____

_____

_____

_____

_____

_____

_____

_____

_____

_____

_____

Who Is Kimberly Kirberger?

Kimberly Kirberger is the president and founder of I.A.M. for Teens, Inc. (Inspiration and Motivation for Teens, Inc.), a corporation formed exclusively to work *for* teens. It is her goal to see teens represented in a more positive light; her strong belief is that teens deserve better and more positive treatment.

She spends her time reading the thousands of letters and stories sent to her by teen readers and traveling around the country speaking to high school students and parents of teens. She has appeared as a teen expert on many television and radio shows, including *Geraldo*, MSNBC, and the *Terry Bradshaw Show*.

Kimberly is the coauthor of the bestselling *Chicken Soup for the Teenage Soul*, the *New York Times* #1 bestselling *Chicken Soup for the Teenage Soul II*, the bestselling *Chicken Soup for the College Soul*, as well as *Chicken Soup for the Teenage Soul Journal*. She is also the coauthor of the forthcoming *Chicken Soup for the Parent's Soul* and *Chicken Soup for the Teenage Soul III*, and the author of *Teen Love: On Relationships*, the first volume in the *Teen Love* series.

Kimberly started the Teen Letter Project with Jack Canfield, Mark Victor Hansen and Health Communications, Inc. The

199

Project is responsible for answering the heartfelt letters received from teenagers and also for reaching out to teens in trouble and encouraging them to seek professional help.

To book Kimberly for a speaking engagement or for further information on any of her projects, please contact:

I.A.M. for Teens, Inc.
P.O. Box 936 ▪ Pacific Palisades, CA 90272
e-mail for stories: *stories@love4teens.com*
e-mail for letters: *letters@love4teens.com*
e-mail for questions and/or submissions
for the *Teen Love* series: *kim@love4teens.com*
Web site: *www.love4teens.com*

Who Is Colin?

Colin Mortensen is a nineteen-year-old Southern California native who is a current cast member on MTV's *The Real World Hawaii* and former host of *The Real World/Road Rules Casting Special 1999*. Colin is an actor and was recently cast as "A. J." in the upcoming NBC comedy series *MYOB*. Colin is using his "popularity" as an opportunity to convey positive images and ideas to young adults.

Prior to being a cast member on *The Real World Hawaii* and hosting *The Casting Special*, Colin completed two years of studies at the University of California at Berkeley. At U. C. Berkeley, Colin was a member of the radio station's sports department. As an on-air personality, Colin performed play-by-play and color-commentary duties for Cal football and men's and women's basketball, anchored the sportscasts daily, and hosted a thirty-minute interview program with various Cal athletes.

Colin has been involved in community service throughout his life, donating his time and clothes, lending an ear to a friend, and volunteering for Special Olympics in high school. Colin speaks to high school and college students around the nation about various subjects concerning young adults. He feels that now that he is in the "public eye," he has a good platform to present young adults with healthy messages and advice about their lives. Because he is a young adult, it is very easy for other young people to relate to his experiences in life. To book Colin for a speaking engagement, please contact:

I.A.M. for Teens, Inc.
P.O. Box 936
Pacific Palisades, CA 90272
phone: 310-573-3655
fax: 310-573-3657

Supporting Teens in Love

Teen Letter Project

We will be expanding the Teen Letter Project to support teens in love. We are setting up a teen staff to answer questions and give support. They will be encouraged to share their own experiences with you and help you know you are not alone.

Teen Love Trees

We have all been aware lately of the problems we are having because of the lack of trees. Since we use trees to make these books, we want to replace them. We thought it would be a great idea for teens to plant a tree to mark their first love. If you wish to participate in this program, please contact our office and we will inform you of how to proceed.

It is the goal of Teen Love Projects to show the world the power and beauty of teen love. A percentage of the profits from this book and the other books in the *Teen Love* series will go to charities that are making a difference in a loving and compassionate way—and using the help of teenagers to do so.

Contributors

Christina Atkinson is a high school senior. She enjoys acting, as well as playing lacrosse and piano. She is involved in her school's student government and is always busy. She thanks her family for everything, always. She can be reached at *Buggynini@aol.com*.

Kristen Keys is a high school junior in Michigan. She works on the yearbook for her school. Some of her favorite things to do are to snow ski, write and hang out with her friends. She plans to become an English teacher and maybe take photos in her spare time.

Rikki Knies is a seventeen-year-old girl who lives in Kamloops, British Columbia, Canada. She lives with her mom, dad and younger sister, Brooke. Rikki loves to read and write poetry, and hopes to publish her own book one day. She can be reached a *rikkik@kamloops.net*.

Nellie McDowell grew up in rural Texas with five brothers and five sisters, and is currently staying busy chasing after her own kids, Cory, Steven and Roni Kay, with her husband, Ron. All of whom, by the way, have been the inspiration for her poems and stories.

Sara Nachtman was so impressed with the response to her piece in *Chicken Soup for the Teenage Soul II* that it encouraged her to keep writing. She graduated high school this past June and is currently attending the University of Northern Iowa. She is majoring in biology and minoring in both French and English. She also plans to swim competitively for the UNI swim team. Sara can be reached at *swmnachts@aol.com*.

Public Service Announcement is a hip-hop group from Berkeley, California that promotes positivity, cultural unity and good old-fashioned love. They are a performance group and also teach workshops at schools and colleges. They can be reached by calling 510-558-1269.

Danielle Rosenblatt is a fifteen-year-old student who enjoys theater, dancing, running, writing and laughing with her friends. She plans to pursue writing as a career and hopes to one day publish her own book. Danielle would like to thank her family and friends, who have filled her life with love and encouraged her to reach for her dreams.

Rebecca Scida is a nineteen-year-old college student. She attends the Indiana University of Pennsylvania, where she is and English major, with a minor in journalism. She loves reading and writing and aspires for a career as a well-respected author.

Permissions *(continued from page iv)*

Endless Love/End Less Love. Reprinted by permission of Kyle Canfield, Joe Gray and Marlon Ingram. ©1999 Kyle Canfield, Joe Gray and Marlon Ingram.

The Road to Love. Reprinted by permission of Lindsey Hartman. ©1999 Lindsey Hartman.

Introduction to *How Odd a Feeling.* Reprinted by permission of Raymond Jones. ©1999 Raymond Jones.

How Odd a Feeling. Reprinted by permission of Rikki Knies. ©1999 Rikki Knies.

Love. Reprinted by permission of Danielle Rosenblatt. ©1999 Danielle Rosenblatt.

No Complaints. Reprinted by permission of Christina Atkinson. ©1999 Christina Atkinson.

Your Game. Reprinted by permission of Rebecca Scida. ©1999 Rebecca Scida.

The Way You . . . Reprinted by permission of Kristen Keys. ©1999 Kristen Keys.

A Heart Too Soft. Reprinted by permission of Nellie McDowell. ©1999 Nellie McDowell.

From Best Selling Author Kim Kirberger

Teen Love - On Relationships

Love! The mystery! At times painful, at times glorious — always a challenge!

#1 New York Times
BESTSELLING AUTHOR
Kimberly Kirberger
*Chicken Soup for the Teenage Soul series
and Teenage Soul Journal*

Teen Love™ Series

On Relationships

A Book for Teenagers

The companion to The Journal, this book will help you look at and understand the myriad of feelings and experiences our relationships put us through.

These accounts of love by and for teens, along with letters and advice will bring you closer to understanding your own confusions and your own passions, as well as those around you.

Code #7346 Quality Paperback • $12.95